OCEAN WORLD

CONTENTS

WHY IS OUR PLANET BLUE?

Our planet looks blue when seen from outer space because nearly three-quarters of Earth is covered by water. Our oceans support an enormous range of life, both above and below the surface — from hordes of seabirds to the fish of the deep.

In this book, you will read about creatures from all over our planet. Use the globes to find the part of the world where these animals live.

Some words in this book are shown in **bold**. Explanations for these words, as they are used in this book, are given in the Glossary on pages 63 and 64.

WELCOME TO THE JOURNEY

The oceans affect every aspect of our lives. They influence our weather and provide an important source of food. The sea is both destroyer and provider; powerful enough to wreck ships with its waves, and gentle enough to provide a home for the tiniest sea creatures. Yet, despite the importance of the oceans, they remain mysterious. We have reached the moon, but the deepest parts of our oceans have hardly been explored.

Beginning with the shore, this book will journey into deeper and deeper waters, eventually reaching 13,000 feet below the surface, where some remarkable discoveries have been made.

Life in the Sea

From the warm, shallow waters around the coasts to the frozen oceans at the poles, the sea teems with life. Plants and animals can survive even in the deepest parts of the ocean, where it is dark and bitterly cold.

The smallest life-form in the sea, **plankton**, is an essential part of the diet of many sea creatures. Plankton is the name for plants and animals so tiny that they are swept to every part of the ocean by the **currents**. They provide a nutritious food source for other creatures. At the water's surface, **schools** of fish eat the plankton. The fish, in turn, are eaten by bigger **predators**; these predators are then eaten by even bigger creatures, and so the process continues. This is called a **food chain**.

school of anchovetta

Plant plankton is vital to life on land as well as in the oceans — it produces 80 percent of the oxygen in the air we breathe. The oxygen is released when the plant plankton makes its own food.

right: striped marlin and school of fish

A World of Facts

Did you know?

🐟 The average depth of the oceans is nearly 2.5 miles, but the average height of land is a little more than a half mile above sea level. There is a vast underwater world that remains unexplored by humans.

🐟 There are mountain ranges underwater. The Mid-Atlantic Ridge is a chain of mountains in the middle of the Atlantic Ocean, extending more than 10,000 miles. That's nearly twice as long as the Andes Mountains in South America.

Record breakers

🐟 The largest ocean is the Pacific, which covers about one-third of Earth's surface. Measuring about 64,000,000 square miles, the Pacific is larger than all the continents combined.

🐟 The Pacific is also the deepest ocean. Its average depth is 14,000 feet, but it reaches down as far as 36,000 feet.

🐟 The blue whale is the largest animal ever to have lived, bigger even than the largest known dinosaur. A blue whale can weigh more than a group of 1,500 people. Its blood vessels are so big that a trout could swim through them, and its heart is as big as a small car.

Strange but true!

🐟 An undersea waterfall beneath the Denmark Straight sinks for more than 2 miles — more than three times the drop of the highest waterfall on land, the Angel Falls in Venezuela.

🐟 The mighty Amazon River is longer and carries more water than any other river on land. But the underwater "river," the Antarctic Circumpolar Current that flows around the continent of Antarctica, is the largest water flow in the world.

ON THE EDGE

Coastlines are the frontiers between land and sea. They are the most dynamic of all the ocean habitats. Coastlines include sandy beaches and rocky cliffs, as well as the coral reefs and **mangrove** swamps of the tropics. Some animals, such as land crabs, spend their whole lives at the coastline. Others, such as turtles, are just visiting. These creatures may have been washed ashore by accident, or traveled there on purpose to feed or breed. Either way, they will not stay long, and will soon return to their real home, the sea.

Life by the Sea

Each spring, when seabirds come ashore to breed, coastlines become like noisy, bustling cities. Funk Island, off the coast of Newfoundland, Canada, attracts gannets, puffins, guillemots, and other seabirds. The birds crowd together in large colonies, jostling for a space on the cliff face where they can lay their eggs. There is safety in numbers; together, the birds are safer, because predators don't want to risk possible attack by hundreds of birds at once.

gannets

Every available space is filled with nests made of sticks and seaweed. Competition for space and food is fierce. When the blue gannet eggs hatch, there are thousands of chicks, naked and black-skinned, needing to be fed. For about three months, the gannet parents journey to and from the sea, bringing back tiny fish for their hungry broods. Then, the parents abandon their young. Hunger drives the parents back to deeper water, where they can dive for fish. The chicks must leave the cliffs to go in search of their own food.

puffins

Mammals of the Sea

walrus

Some sea **mammals** spend their whole lives at sea, but not walruses, seals, and sea lions. These mammals live in freezing waters that are far too harsh for their newborn pups, so the animals come ashore to breed. Their pups remain on land until they have enough fat on their bodies to stay warm in the icy seas.

Like the seabirds, sea mammals breed in huge colonies. In Antarctica, up to 10,000 elephant seals may squeeze onto a single beach each spring. There are reasons for this crowding. As the seabirds found, predators are unlikely to attack a large crowd. Also, the animals can find and choose a mate much more easily on the crowded beach than in the open sea.

seal pup

Turtles at Risk

Turtles also come ashore to breed. They choose sandy beaches where they bury their eggs, and usually return to the beach on which they were born. About half the world's population of flatbacked turtles gathers each year on Crab Island, off the coast of Australia. The turtles bury their soft, leathery eggs in the sand and then hurry back to the sea.

Olive Ridley turtle

baby turtle being
eaten by a gull

When they hatch, the baby turtles must struggle down to the safety of the
water, but predators, such as seabirds, are waiting to pounce. Nearly half of
the baby flatbacks are killed and eaten each year.

The Olive Ridley turtle tries to overcome its predators by sheer
numbers. Over a span of just three nights, approximately 100,000
of them come to the same beach to lay their eggs. Many hatch–
lings will still be eaten, but some will survive.

A World of Facts

Did you know?

- Turtles can live to be more than 100 years old.

- Turtles don't have teeth — they have sharp beaks that they use for biting.

- Puffins nest in burrows on grassy cliff tops. Sometimes, puffins dig their own burrows — but if they find an empty rabbit hole, they may take that over, instead.

- Guillemots live in huge, crowded colonies of more than 140,000 birds.

Record breakers

- The world's largest sea turtle is the leatherback, which can grow to 6 feet long and weigh more than 1,100 pounds.

Strange but true!

- The sex of a turtle hatchling depends on the temperature of the sand. Where the sand is warm, the turtle will be female. Where the sand is cool, the turtle will be male.

- Walruses and seals spend most of their lives at sea, but they enjoy sunbathing on the beach in summer.

BETWEEN THE TIDES

There is a force powerful enough to move the oceans of the world. It is a force generated by the moon, 230,000 miles away. As the moon orbits Earth, its **gravity** sweeps across the face of our planet, creating tides. Tides are the regular rise and fall of the sea. A high tide occurs when the gravity of the moon pulls on the part of the sea that is nearest to it, which causes a low tide somewhere else. On the shore, the portion of the beach between low and high tides is covered and uncovered by the sea twice a day. This makes life difficult for the creatures that live there. At high tide, they can move around in relative safety but at low tide, the hot sun could dry them out, or wading birds could eat them. They need to find ways of protecting themselves.

Tidal Dangers

The movement of water in tidal areas creates huge waves and fierce currents. At low tide, shellfish and other tide-pool creatures are swept out to sea, creating rich feeding grounds for herring, whales, dolphins, and seabirds. Some creatures, such as clams, sand eels, and crabs, bury themselves in the sand during low tide, while others, such as limpets and mussels, close up their shells and cling tightly to the rocks.

The Sally Lightfoot crab, found on the rocky shorelines of Central and South America, has a flattened shell so that it can squeeze into narrow spaces between the rocks and avoid being washed away. When the tide comes in, the crabs come out of hiding and scuttle around, looking for food.

Sally Lightfoot crab

Food for Free

raccoon

The beach can provide a good hunting ground for hungry land animals. When a very low tide uncovers the large, deepwater crabs on Vancouver Island, Canada, raccoons come down to the beach for a feast. The raccoons are able to crack open the crab shells and enjoy a tasty meal. In southeastern Alaska, grizzly bears dig in the sand for clams.

Colonies of garden eels live tail-down in burrows in the sand. They push their heads and necks out of the burrows to feed on passing plankton, leaving the rest of their bodies buried beneath the seabed. When they all go out feeding together, they look like a field of waving grass. The slightest disturbance from an approaching predator will send the eels back to their burrows. They will only appear again when they're sure it's safe.

garden eels

Tropical Waters

Tides vary from place to place. Geographical position determines the level of the tide. In the warm, tropical waters around Florida and the Caribbean, the tides are gentle. One of nature's oddest creatures lives here — a large but harmless mammal called the manatee.

Manatees are sometimes called sea cows, and it is easy to see why — they graze on seagrass and other plants of the shallow waters. Manatees need to eat around 10 percent of their body weight each day — that's about 175 pounds of food. They can live in both fresh and salt water, as long as it's warm.

tropical waters, Bahamas

manatee

Sadly, the manatee is an endangered species. In Florida, there are only about 1,900 of these animals left. This is mainly due to the destruction of seagrass beds caused by pollution and coastal development. Manatees are now protected by international law.

A World of Facts

Did you know?

🐟 The flow of water in and out of the Bay of Fundy in Canada is the largest tidal movement in the world — the difference between high and low tide can be as much as 52 feet.

🐟 A manatee's front teeth are worn down by constant grinding on seagrass. New teeth grow in the back of the manatee's mouth and gradually replace all the old ones.

🐟 After the rains on Christmas Island, near Australia, millions of red crabs march from the forests to the sea. They wait on the shore until the tides are right for carrying their eggs to the open ocean. Then they swarm into the sea to **spawn**.

Record breakers

🐟 The largest crab on record is a Japanese giant spider crab, which weighed 40 pounds.

🐟 The biggest **jellyfish** species in the world, the lion's mane jellyfish, is found in the North Atlantic Ocean and the Arctic Ocean. Its body can measure 7.8 feet across, and each tentacle can be more than 108 feet long.

Strange but true!

🐟 Mudskippers are fish that can survive in water and on land. They live in the mudflats of tropical **estuaries**. When in the water, the mudskipper breathes through its gills. It stores water in its gill chambers and this supplies the oxygen it needs when it's out of the water. Mudskippers can breathe through their skin.

🐟 Male fiddler crabs have one huge claw and one small claw. They wave the large claw in the air to attract the attention of females, and they feed themselves with the smaller claw. Fiddler crabs live on the beaches of **temperate** and tropical regions of the world.

THE CORAL SEAS

Coral reefs are found in shallow tropical seas. They are made by millions of tiny animals called coral **polyps**, living together in colonies. Each polyp has a soft body with a mouth at the top, ringed by stinging tentacles. Its skeleton is on the outside, and looks like a little limestone cup. **Algae**, aquatic plants including seaweed, provide food for the polyps, which, in turn, provide shelter for the algae. When coral polyps eventually die, live coral grows on top of them, forming a thin layer of color over the dead coral's white skeleton.

next page: a coral reef

Active Nightlife

Like a big city, the reef is awake and active all night long. As the sea becomes dark, the night shift takes over. This is when many of the predators hunt. Some fish change color at night, becoming darker so predators can't easily spot them. Moray eels slither around the coral, seeking out their prey by smell. White-tipped sharks use their special electrical sense to detect the slight movements of sleeping fish.

white-tipped sharks

Most corals
feed at night when
there are fewer fish
around to nibble
their tentacles.
When corals
catch passing
animal plankton,
they paralyze their prey
using stinging cells.

Coral polyps can share their
meals — the stomach cavities
of all of the coral polyps are
connected, so they can pass
food along to one another.

coral

Terrorist of the Reef

coral polyps

Even though coral polyps live inside hard skeletons, they are not safe from attack. The most vicious killer of coral is the crown-of-thorns starfish. One of the world's largest starfish, it can grow up to 31 inches across.

crown-of-thorns starfish

This dangerous creature has between six and twenty-three arms, all bristling with **toxic** spines and lined with hundreds of suckers. It settles on a coral reef, turns its stomach inside out, and eats the polyps in huge quantities. When the starfish moves on, only the coral skeleton is left. In four to six hours, a starfish can eat a patch the size of a dinner plate. A single crown-of-thorns starfish can eat more than 54 square yards of coral in one year. Although the coral polyps cannot run away, they do put up a fight by stinging the starfish. Crabs and shrimp also come to their aid by pinching the predator until it goes away.

A World of Facts

Did you know?

🐟 Corals have existed for approximately 400 million years.

🐟 Coral reefs are found off the shores of more than 100 countries. Worldwide, coral reefs are thought to cover nearly 175,000 square miles.

🐟 The biggest threat to coral reefs is not the hungry crown of thorns starfish, but people. Overfishing is one problem; people who collect coral to sell as ornaments is another.

Record breakers

🐟 The Australian Great Barrier Reef is the largest coral structure in the world. It is really a chain of reefs that stretches across nearly 1,500 miles.

🐟 The biggest type of coral is the mushroom coral. It is a single polyp that can grow to nearly 10 inches across. It is mobile, able to move along the seabed and turn itself right side up if a storm knocks it down.

🐟 One of the largest inhabitants of a reef is the giant clam — it can reach more than 4.5 feet in length.

Strange but true!

🐟 Coral is easily destroyed — even brushing against it can kill it. The anchor of one cruise ship can destroy an area of reef as big as two Olympic swimming pools.

🐟 Scientists consider the Great Barrier Reef to be young — even though it is 10,000 years old!

THE TEMPERATE SEAS

The temperate seas lie between the polar zones of the Arctic and Antarctic oceans and the tropical regions near the equator. These waters are home to large seaweeds. The giant of the seaweed world is the kelp that forms underwater forests off the coast of California. Kelp **fronds** can grow to more than 325 feet in length and provide an ideal home for shoals of fish.

The warm summer sunshine also enables vast "blooms" of plant plankton to grow. Summer is a time of plenty, but when winter arrives, the water becomes too cold for new plankton to grow or develop. Heavy storms sweep the existing plankton out to sea. Facing such harsh conditions and a lack of available food, many animals swim to warmer waters. They will return when summer comes again.

The Seals of Sable Island

It is January. The seas around Sable Island, Canada, are cold, gray, and stormy. The air is full of the sounds and smells of gray seals, thousands of whom are dragging themselves onto the beaches. Despite the harsh weather conditions, this is the breeding season for the gray seal.

gray seals

seal pup

For the seals, breeding in winter is not a gamble, but a sensible survival plan. The mother seals have spent the autumn months fattening up on fish, and now they are in top condition. For the first 18 days of their lives, the seal pups will feed on their mother's milk. After that, they must survive on their own blubber until they are ready to go to sea, several weeks later. By the time they are able to hunt for themselves, spring will have arrived, and the food supplies will return.

Herrings and Killer Whales

On the eastern side of the Atlantic, vast shoals of herring have swum into the cold waters of the Norwegian **fjords** to seek shelter from the stormy winter seas. The local fishermen know the fish are there, and each winter they gather a plentiful harvest.

Out at sea, another group of fishermen is waiting — a **pod** of killer whales, or orcas. These streamlined mammals have been stalking the herring for months, eating great quantities of the oily fish.

Killer whales have a wide diet. Apart from herring and other fish, they catch and eat dolphins, seals, and even seabirds and turtles if they can get them. Killer whales can swim huge distances, and are found in every ocean of the world.

killer whale pod, Norway

March of the Lobsters

Midsummer has arrived, and the waters of Canada's Atlantic coast are now warmer. But out in the deep, it is still cold — and an army is on the march. This is a column of giant female Atlantic lobsters, each weighing up to 22 pounds — though some record breakers have grown to 44 pounds. The lobsters are heading for the warm, shallow, coastal waters to spawn. Each lobster can carry between 10,000 and 30,000 eggs.

In the sea, every creature is a meal for some other living thing, and even the heavily armored lobster is not safe. The baby lobsters, too, no bigger than plankton, will be sought out by greedy fish. Only very few of the vast numbers of eggs will hatch. Even fewer will survive to grow big enough to move back to the deep oceans.

Atlantic lobster

A World of Facts

Did you know?

- Sea otters living in kelp forests sleep on the surface of the water. They twist a strand of kelp around their bodies to anchor them and ensure they don't get swept out to sea.

- Lobsters can live to be more than sixty years old.

Record breakers

- In March of each year, kelp becomes the fastest-growing plant on Earth. It can grow as much as 24 inches a day.

- The killer whale is the biggest member of the dolphin family. It can grow to nearly 32 feet long.

- Atlantic lobsters can weigh up to 44 pounds, but most weigh about 2 pounds.

Strange but true!

- Killer whales have been known to come up onto a beach to snatch seals.

- Alginates, chemicals produced from kelp, are used in around seventy everyday items including toothpaste and candy. They are even used to thicken ice cream and paint.

FROZEN WATERS

The frozen seas of the Arctic and Antarctic regions seem a cruel and impossible habitat — and yet they are teeming with life. The Arctic and Antarctic are very different from each other. The Antarctic is a frozen continent surrounded by icy seas, while the Arctic is a frozen sea surrounded by land. The animals that live in these two places are different, too, but they share similar survival problems.

Emperor Penguins

It is early winter on the Antarctic Ice Sheet. It is dark, and the temperature is −58°F. A 62-mile-per-hour wind is blowing. Without protection, a human being would be dead in minutes. It seems almost impossible for anything to live on these frozen wastes and yet, huddled together for warmth, a colony of emperor penguins is waiting for their chicks to hatch.

It is the male emperor penguins that keep the eggs warm; they balance the eggs on their feet and protect them under a pouch of skin. The penguins have developed a special way of keeping out of the worst of the biting wind. The birds are always shuffling around, taking turns standing on the side of the group that is sheltered from the wind — all the time carrying their one egg balanced on their feet.

As the eggs hatch in the summer, the females return from the sea, each carrying the first meal for its newborn chick in its beak. At last, the hungry males are able to swim out to sea for food. For the next few months, the males and females will take turns feeding and guarding the chicks.

emperor penguins with chick

43

Polar Bears

Conditions in the Antarctic might be the toughest in the world, but at least there are no land-based predators. Creatures of the Arctic, such as seals, walruses, and small whales, must be very careful. Once they are trapped, a polar bear's powerful paws can kill them with a single blow.

A sudden freeze has trapped a beluga whale beneath the Arctic ice. A polar bear has spotted it. The stranded whale will not last long.

Seals protect their pups as best they can by hiding them in ice caves or breeding on **ice floes** beyond the reach of polar bears. Even so, only when the ice melts are they reasonably safe from an attack by this dreaded predator. Polar bears can smell meat up to 20 miles away and a polar bear's stomach can hold 20 percent of its body weight.

right: polar bear
next page: humpback whales

A World of Facts

Did you know?

🐟 Polar bears have hair between the pads of their feet to help them get a better grip when running on the ice.

🐟 Although they cannot fly in the air, penguins "fly" underwater at speeds of nearly 20 miles per hour.

Record breakers

🐟 The polar bear is the world's largest land meat-eater. A male polar bear stands up to 9.5 feet tall on his hind legs, and weighs nearly 900 pounds.

🐟 A newborn polar bear cub is about 1 foot long, only slightly bigger than a rat.

🐟 Humpback whales can grow to nearly 70 feet long and weigh more than 70 tons.

🐟 Emperor penguins are the largest of all penguins, growing to three feet in height and weighing up to 70 pounds.

Strange but true!

🐟 Most of the time, polar bears move slowly to avoid overheating, but they can swim at nearly 6 miles per hour.

🐟 Beneath its white fur, a polar bear's skin is actually black.

THE OPEN OCEAN

For creatures that make their homes in the open sea, the world must seem a lonely place. The vast, empty ocean stretches from **horizon** to horizon and, apart from scattered islands, the nearest land may be hundreds of miles away. Even the seabed may be more than five miles below the surface. There is little plankton out here and, without this, the food chain cannot get started. Such food as there is can be swept away easily by giant storms. Yet, even here, animals survive. "Hot spots" of plankton appear and long-distance travelers such as the blue shark will cross the whole distance of the Atlantic Ocean to find food.

Cocos Island

Like deserts on land, the open ocean is a habitat where shelter is scarce. Deserts have oases, places with water and plants where travelers can rest. The open oceans have islands that provide a living and resting space for the ocean's travelers. Cocos Island, 100 miles from the South American coast, is an extinct volcano. For long-distance travelers, the island is like a highway rest stop, where they can fill up with a meal.

Cocos Island

a young masked booby

The island provides a roost site for boobies, birds that scour the sea for schools of bait fish.

Swirling currents concentrate the plankton here. Fish come to feed on the plankton, predators such as sharks come to feed on the fish — and so the food chain builds.

plant plankton floating in the sea

Hitching a Ride

The oceans are full of hitchhikers. On the coast of California, mats of floating kelp drift hundreds of miles out to sea. Each seaweed raft carries a small colony of life. Even a floating log can provide an ocean cruise for a colony of sea barnacles. Barnacles and other **parasites** also cluster on creatures such as whales — and hitch a free ride around the world.

bowhead whale

manta ray

compass jellyfish

Fish hitchhike, too. Small fish hide from predators among the tentacles of stinging jellyfish. Remora, or suckerfish, use their suckers to stick themselves to manta rays or whale sharks, so they don't need to swim.

The only problem with hitching a ride is being unable to choose where to go. For plankton, the journey often leads them right into the mouths of a hungry creature.

Dolphins

Dolphins are the great high jumpers of the open ocean. This behavior is called **porpoising**. It is a very efficient way of traveling vast distances across the ocean. In the air, the dolphins don't have to push against water resistance, and they are able to breathe freely and continue moving at high speed.

Passengers on ocean liners often see dolphins following or swimming alongside the ship, and sometimes imagine they are simply being friendly. But this isn't the case. The dolphins are saving energy, letting the **bow wave** of the ship pull them along. Dolphins surf, using the pressure created when the front of a moving ship pushes through the water.

spinner dolphins underwater

A World of Facts

Did you know?

➤ The word *plankton* comes from a Greek word, *planktos*, and means "drifting."

➤ Australia's box jellyfish is the most dangerous jellyfish. Its toxin is stronger than cobra venom and can kill a person in minutes.

➤ Dolphins can dive down to more than 1,000 feet and can jump up to 20 feet out of the water.

Record breakers

➤ When early sailors crossed the Atlantic and Pacific oceans, they thought they saw sea monsters. Perhaps they saw the longest fish in the world, the oarfish, which can grow to a length of 20 feet or more. The oarfish has a long, red fin, a horselike face, and blue gills.

➤ The world's largest fish, whale sharks, feed almost exclusively on plankton.

Strange but true!

➤ Dolphins make a noise about fourteen times higher-pitched than humans can hear. When the sound waves hit an underwater object, the dolphins can use the echoes produced to locate the object and find out whether it is suitable food.

➤ Jellyfish are made up of more than 95 percent water and have no heart, bones, or brain, and no real eyes. They have sensors to let them know whether they are heading up or down.

THE DEEP

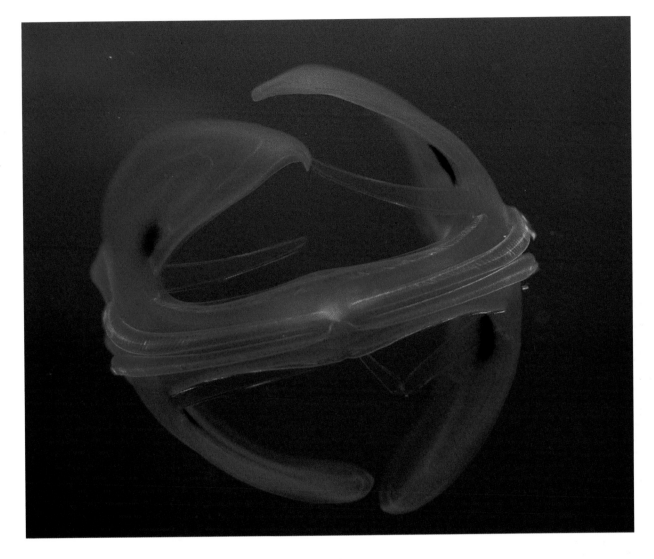

Much of the sea is more than a half mile deep. Most of this is completely unexplored — only a few submarines can reach the very deepest parts. By 30 feet down, the **water pressure** has doubled, and the light starts to fade. At 600 feet below the surface, it's almost completely dark and the water is very cold. This is known as the "twilight zone." By 3,000 feet, all light has gone and the pressure is immense. Yet, even here, strange forms of life can thrive.

The Twilight Zone

squid

The trick to survival in the twilight zone is to avoid being eaten — by not being seen. Creatures here try to make themselves invisible. Some animals have transparent bodies that are hard to see in the dim light. Even larger creatures such as squid make themselves as see-through as possible. Down here, everyone is a master of disguise.

A hatchet fish confuses enemies with its mirrorlike, flattened sides. But predators will find ways to track down a meal. Many have developed large, extra-sensitive eyes to make the best use of the faint light.

hatchet fish

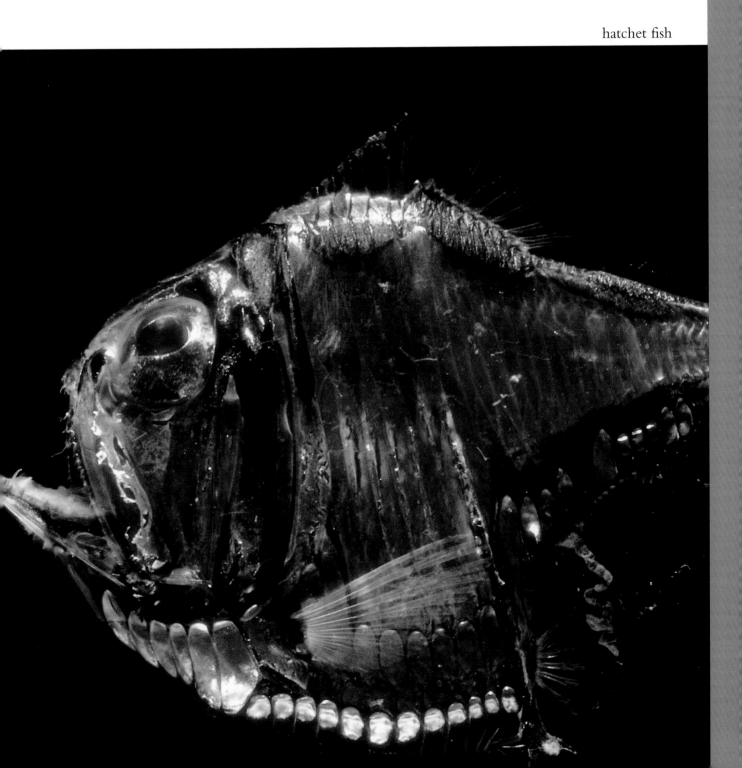

The Dark Zone

Below 3,000 feet, all sunlight is gone. This is an alien world of total darkness. To survive here, in the "dark zone," creatures have had to develop senses other than sight, as well as a few amazing tricks.

Some of the creatures produce a tiny amount of light themselves. This is called **bioluminescence**. Lantern fish have light-producing areas on their skin and can flash messages to one another in a mysterious Morselike code of their own. The female anglerfish grows a "fishing rod" at the front of her head. A light dangles at the end of this to attract her next meal. This creature has also solved the problem of finding a mate — the male anglerfish has a super-sensitive "nose" that can sniff out a distant female.

anglerfish

60

right: hungry anglerfish

A World of Facts

Did you know?

🐟 Until 1930, the greatest ocean depth reached by humans was approximately 600 feet.

🐟 In 1934, a record-breaking dive reached approximately 2,500 feet using a **bathysphere**.

🐟 In 1960, people reached a depth of 35,800 feet. This is still the deepest recorded dive of a submersible craft with people inside.

🐟 Ocean water is always coldest at the bottom where it is usually between 39.2°F and 30.2°F.

Record breakers

🐟 The deepest place on Earth is the Mariana Trench at the bottom of the Challenger Deep in the Pacific Ocean. This trench is 36,161 feet deep.

Strange but true!

🐟 Some deep-sea creatures are able to turn red, to protect themselves from predators. The color red is difficult to see in deep water and makes the animals nearly invisible.

🐟 Anglerfish have teeth in their throats to prevent their prey from escaping.

GLOSSARY

Alga Any one of many simple, nonflowering plants found in water. Seaweeds are algae.

Bathysphere A chamber that is lowered into the sea by a cable attached to a ship. Scientists can observe ocean plants and animals from inside it.

Bioluminescence Light produced by living things.

Bow wave A wave created by a ship moving quickly through the water.

Current A body of water moving in one direction. Ocean currents are affected by the forces of gravity and wind direction.

Estuary A water passage where the tide meets a river current.

Fjord A deep valley carved long ago by a glacier and then filled with seawater.

Food chain The feeding pattern in any particular place, where plants and small creatures feed bigger animals, which in turn feed even bigger animals.

Frond The leaf or leaflike part of a palm, fern, or similar plant.

Gravity The force that pulls an object towards the center of the earth, or any other mass.

Horizon The line where the land (or sea) and sky seem to meet.

Ice floes A flat, floating area of ice.

Jellyfish A marine animal that has a jellylike, transparent circular body with stinging tentacles around the edge.

Mammal An animal that has hair, and gives birth to and nurses live young.

Mangrove A woody plant that grows between the sea and the land in areas where there are tides.

Parasite A living thing that survives, to its advantage, on or in another living thing.

Plankton Microscopic plants and animals that float in the sea.

Pod A small herd or school of marine animals, especially whales.

Polyp The living part of a coral. When it dies, the polyp leaves behind a chalky shell that gradually builds up to make a coral reef.

Porpoising Traveling through the water by alternately rising above it and then submerging.

Predator An animal that kills other creatures for food.

School A large number of fish swimming together.

Spawn Releasing huge quantities of eggs or sperm into the water.

Temperate The part of the world that lies between the tropical and polar zones, where temperatures are moderate or mild. In temperate seas, the surface temperature averages around 68°F.

Toxic Poisonous.

Water pressure The force of water pushing against an object.

Text by David Orme and Helen Bird
The publishers wish to thank the following for the use of pictures:
The BBC Natural History Unit pp: 1, 12tl, 43, 64 (Doug Allen); 34, 35 (Penny Allen); 26–27, 30–31, 32, 33, 63, 64 (Georgette Douwma); 29, 30tl (Steve Downer); 41 (Hanne and Jens Eriksen); 8, 44 (Sue Flood); 4–5 (Alistair Fothergill); 12–13 (Jeff Foott); 36–37, 42, 52–53 (Martha Holmes); 10-11,14–15, 16, 46–47, 63 (Ben Osborne); 17, 18–19, 24 (Pete Oxford); 20, 22-23, 63 (Hugh Pearson); 21, 23tr, 25, 53, 56, 57 (Michael Pitts); 28 (Jeff Rotman); 50 (John Ruthven); 49, 51b, 58, 59, 60, 61, 62, 64 (David Shale); 38–39, 40 (Peter Scoones); 45 (Staffan Widstrand)

And also: Florian Graner pp: 9, 51t, 54t, 63; Didier Noirot p:11tr; David Reichert pp: 6, 7, 54–55.